Patagonia Guide 2024

Exploration: Your Updated Guide to Top Attractions with Must See Sights and Hidden Gems- Be there; Epic Adventure Travels to see Enchanting Unspoiled Wilderness Trip.

Rick Paul

Disclaimer Notice

The information in this document is for educational and entertainment purposes only. No warranties, explicit or implied, are made. The author is not providing legal, financial, medical, or professional advice. Consult licensed professionals for guidance before implementing any techniques. The author is not liable for any losses or damages resulting from the use of this information. By accessing and reading this document, the reader agrees to hold the author harmless from any direct or indirect losses or damages resulting from the use of the information provided herein. The author shall not be held liable for errors, omissions, or inaccuracies present in the content. Each reader is solely responsible for the decisions they make based on the information presented in this document.

Introduction

In the southernmost reaches of the South American continent lies a land that defies imagining. A land of jagged peaks and glaciers, where condors soar through cobalt skies and penguins parade along rugged coasts. A land where untamed wilderness stretches as far as the eye can see, and the pulse of nature beats unrelenting. This is Patagonia, a realm of wonder and awe, where the lines between dreams and reality blur.

As I stood at the precipice of my Patagonian journey, I couldn't help but feel a sense of trepidation and joy coursing through my veins. The very name "Patagonia" conjures pictures of pristine landscapes, ancient woods, and raw, unfiltered beauty. It's a place that draws adventurers, a place that calls to those who yearn for the untamed, the uncharted.

My love affair with Patagonia started long before I set foot on its hallowed ground. It started with photographs, tales of exploration, and whispered legends of a land where nature rules supreme. Each image of towering granite spires and turquoise glacial lakes was a siren's call, drawing me closer to a dream I thought might forever remain unreachable.

But dreams, they have a way of weaving themselves into the weave of reality when one least expects it. And so it was, as I boarded a plane headed for the farthest reaches of South America, that I knew I was stepping into something extraordinary.

The moment I arrived in Buenos Aires, Argentina's bustling city, the air crackled with energy. It was a city of passion and life, where tango rhythms filled the streets, and a thriving arts scene honored the human spirit. But the city's allure, though obvious, couldn't keep my heart from the siren call of Patagonia for long.

From Buenos Aires, I started on a journey southward, towards the heart of Patagonia. My first stop was El Calafate, a small town set on the shores of Lake Argentino. It was the gateway to one of the most amazing natural wonders I had ever encountered: the Perito Moreno Glacier.

As I looked upon the glacier's icy expanse, the world around me seemed to hold its breath. Towering walls of ice rose like ancient sentinels, their cerulean blue hues an otherworldly sight. The glacier moved and groaned, an ever-present reflection of nature's ceaseless rhythm. I walked along the well-maintained walkways, my senses overwhelmed by the magnitude of it all. And as I watched huge chunks of ice calve into the lake with thunderous roars, I knew that Patagonia was a place where one could touch the very soul of the Earth.

But my journey was just starting, for beyond El Calafate lay El Chaltén, a village nestled at the foot of the Andes. It was a place where hikers and mountaineers met, drawn by the promise of untamed wilderness and pristine trails. Here, I started on treks that would take me to the very heart of Patagonia's rugged beauty.

The path to Laguna de los Tres was a revelation. As I hiked through ancient forests and across crystal-clear streams, I felt a deep link to the land. And when I finally reached the viewpoint, I was rewarded with a sight that brought tears to my eyes: the iconic spires of Mount Fitz Roy, their granite peaks kissed by the morning sun. It was a moment of pure, unadulterated awe.

Yet, Patagonia was not just about conquering summits and traversing glaciers. It was a place of profound solitude and thought. In the serene beauty of Laguna Capri, with its mirror-like waters reflecting the nearby peaks, I found a sense of peace that had long eluded me in the chaos of the modern world.

But it was Torres del Paine that would steal my heart completely. The moment I entered the park, I was greeted by the fiery reds and oranges of lenga trees, their leaves ablaze in the fall sun. Guanacos grazed peacefully, and the air was filled with the beautiful calls of birds. It was a place where time seemed to stand still, where the world's worries melted away.

Each day in Torres del Paine brought new wonders. I hiked to the base of the towering Torres themselves, their granite towers rising like mythical giants from the earth. I stood at the shores of Lake Pehoe, looking across its impossibly blue waters to the Cuernos del Paine, their horn-like peaks a testament to nature's artistry. And as I walked along the shores of Lake Grey, I watched massive icebergs drift lazily by, calved from the nearby glacier.

But it was the W Trek that would forever etch itself into my soul. Five days of hiking through some of the world's most beautiful scenery, from the shores of Lake Nordenskjold to the towering heights of the French Valley, each step was a testament to the power and beauty of nature. I watched in awe as condors circled overhead, their beautiful wings catching the wind. And as I reached the viewpoint at the end of the path, the Grey Glacier lay before me, its fractured ice a mesmerizing mosaic of blues and whites.

Yet, amid the grandeur of Patagonia's landscapes, it was the people who left the deepest impact on me. In tiny villages like El Chaltén and Puerto Natales, I met warmth and hospitality that transcended language barriers. I shared meals with locals, listened to their stories, and marveled at their deep relationship to the land.

It was during one such encounter that an idea started to take shape in my mind. I understood that the beauty and wonder of Patagonia should not be the privilege of a fortunate few. It should be available to all who dream of venturing into the wild, of breathing in the crisp mountain air, and of feeling the heartbeat of the Earth beneath their feet.

And so, the seed of this book was planted—a book that would serve as a guide, a friend, and an inspiration for those who yearn to explore Patagonia. It is my hope that these pages will provide useful insights, travel tips, and a glimpse into the soul-stirring experiences that await in this untamed land.

In the chapters that follow, I will share the information I have gained, the lessons I have learned, and the stories I have collected during my Patagonian odyssey. I will guide you through the logistics of planning a trip to Patagonia, from getting there to finding the perfect accommodations and savoring the local food. I will present you to the myriad of activities that await, from glacier trekking to wildlife watching, and from kayaking serene rivers to hiking through ancient forests.

But above all, I will try to convey the essence of Patagonia—the untamed spirit of a land where nature rules supreme, where adventure awaits around every corner, and where the human spirit can find solace and inspiration.

So, dear reader, as you start on this journey through the pages of this book, I invite you to open your heart to Patagonia. Let its grandeur fill your soul, its scenery humble your spirit, and its people warm your heart. And may the stories and insights within these chapters serve as your compass on your own Patagonian odyssey, as you, too, set out to find the untamed.

Contents

Chapter 1: Preparing for Your Patagonian Adventure

Beginning Your Journey

Starting Out: Getting Ready

Embarking on a journey to Patagonia is an exciting prospect, but it requires meticulous preparations to ensure a smooth and enjoyable experience. Here's a closer look at what you need to do to get started:

Passport and Visa

One of the initial steps is to ensure your passport is valid for at least six months beyond your planned departure date. Additionally, research the visa requirements for your specific nationality. Patagonia spans both Chile and Argentina, and visa regulations can differ between the two countries.

Health Precautions

The next crucial consideration is your health. Before traveling, consult with your healthcare provider about necessary vaccinations and health precautions. Depending on your travel plans, you might need protection against diseases such as typhoid, hepatitis A and B, or rabies. Also, ensure you have an adequate supply of any prescription medications you may need during your journey.

Travel Insurance

While Patagonia offers awe-inspiring natural beauty, it's also a place of remote and rugged landscapes. To account for unforeseen circumstances, it's advisable to purchase comprehensive travel insurance. This should cover potential trip cancellations, medical emergencies, and evacuation from remote areas.

Itinerary Planning

Creating a detailed itinerary is vital for a well-organized trip. Outline the destinations you wish to explore, the activities you plan to undertake, and your accommodation preferences. Consider the duration of your stay in each location and allocate time accordingly.

Packing Essentials

Patagonia's diverse landscapes bring with them varying weather conditions. From cold and wet to warm and sunny, you'll encounter it all. Pack accordingly, and don't forget essentials like waterproof clothing, sturdy hiking boots, a good-quality backpack, and insect repellent. Check the specific packing list for each region you intend to visit.

Language

While you'll find English spoken in tourist areas, Patagonia's primary language is Spanish. Familiarizing yourself with some basic Spanish phrases can greatly enhance your experience, as it allows you to connect with locals and navigate the region more easily.

Exploring Patagonia: A Quick Overview

Before diving into the detailed planning, it's helpful to gain a broad understanding of what Patagonia is all about:

Geography

Patagonia is renowned for its vast and diverse landscapes. You'll encounter everything from towering glaciers and jagged mountain ranges to lush forests and crystal-clear lakes. The region's breathtaking natural beauty is a highlight of any visit.

Climate

Patagonia's climate varies widely due to its immense size. In one area, you might experience temperate conditions, while just a few hundred miles away, you could be in a frigid, windswept environment. Be prepared for a wide range of weather, and dress in layers to adapt to changing conditions.

Wildlife

Patagonia is a haven for wildlife enthusiasts. Throughout your journey, keep an eye out for indigenous animals such as guanacos, condors, and the elusive puma. In certain coastal areas, you may even have the opportunity to observe penguins, seals, and whales.

Cultural Diversity

Beyond its natural wonders, Patagonia also boasts a rich cultural heritage. Influenced by indigenous communities and European immigrants, the region's culture is a fascinating blend of traditions, from gaucho (cowboy) culture to indigenous Mapuche influences.

Planning Your Visit

Navigating Patagonia: How to Get There

Getting to Patagonia is an adventure in itself, and the mode of transportation you choose can significantly impact your experience:

Air Travel

For most international travelers, the journey begins by flying to major gateway cities such as Buenos Aires (Argentina) or Santiago (Chile). From these cities, you'll find regular domestic flights connecting to regional airports like El Calafate, Punta Arenas, or Bariloche. Flying is the quickest way to reach Patagonia's key entry points.

Bus Travel

For those who enjoy a more immersive travel experience, long-distance buses offer an economical and scenic option. Buses are known for their comfort, offering reclining seats and even meals on some routes. Traveling by bus allows you to take in the stunning landscapes and make stops along the way to explore.

Car Rental

Renting a car in Patagonia provides unparalleled freedom and flexibility. This option is particularly attractive if you plan to explore remote or less accessible areas. Keep in mind that road conditions can vary, so choose a suitable vehicle and be prepared for different terrains.

Arriving in Patagonia: Your Arrival Options

Upon your arrival in Patagonia, you'll be presented with various entry points, each offering its unique experiences and attractions:

El Calafate:

Ideal For: Those interested in exploring glaciers, including the renowned Perito Moreno Glacier.

Highlights:

- Perito Moreno Glacier: Witness the awe-inspiring sight of this advancing glacier and take the opportunity to walk on its walkways.
- Mini Trekking on Ice: Embark on a thrilling adventure by hiking on the glacier's surface.
- Estancia Nibepo Aike: Experience Patagonian rural life on a full-day program at this traditional estancia.

El Chaltén:

Ideal For: Hikers and nature enthusiasts seeking world-class trekking experiences.

Highlights:

- Cóndor and Eagle Viewpoints: Enjoy panoramic views of

the stunning landscapes.

- Laguna de los Tres: Trek to this picturesque lake for a postcard-worthy view of Mount Fitz Roy.
- Kayaking in Rio de las Vueltas: Explore the region's waterways by kayak for a unique perspective.

Puerto Natales:

Ideal For: A base for exploring Torres del Paine National Park and experiencing the unique culture of the region.

Highlights:

- Salto Grande Waterfall: Marvel at the powerful waterfall within Torres del Paine.
- Visit to Puerto Natales: Discover the town's charm and explore its restaurants and shops.
- Horse Riding in Estancia El Lazo: Experience the Patagonian countryside on horseback.

Punta Arenas:

Ideal For: Those interested in cultural attractions, wildlife encounters, and exploring the Fuegian channels.

Highlights:

- City Tour: Explore Punta Arenas' historical and cultural landmarks.
- Magdalena Island: Visit the iconic Magdalena Island to observe a large penguin colony.
- The King Penguin Colony in Useless Bay: Witness the magnificent king penguins in their natural habitat.

These entry points offer unique experiences and serve as the starting points for your Patagonian adventure. Your choice will depend on your interests and the specific attractions you wish to explore.

Finding the Right Time

Timing is crucial when planning your Patagonian adventure, as the region experiences diverse weather conditions and seasonal changes. Here, we delve into the factors to consider when determining the best time to visit:

Timing Matters: When to Go

Patagonia is a year-round destination, but each season offers distinct advantages and experiences. Your choice depends on your preferences and the activities you want to pursue:

Spring (September to November):

Highlights:

- Wildflowers: Spring brings vibrant wildflowers, painting the landscapes with vivid colors.

- Migratory Birds: Birdwatching enthusiasts can spot various migratory bird species.

- Less Crowds: Fewer tourists, making it an excellent time for a quieter experience.

Considerations:

- Chilly Nights: Nights can still be cold, so pack warm clothing.

- Variable Weather: Weather can be unpredictable, so be prepared for sudden changes.

Summer (December to February):

Highlights:

- Longer Days: Enjoy extended daylight hours for more outdoor activities.

- Mild Temperatures: Pleasant temperatures make for comfortable exploration.

- Wildlife Viewing: Many wildlife species are active, including whales and penguins.

Considerations:

- Peak Tourist Season: Patagonia experiences its highest tourist influx, so book accommodations and tours in advance.

- Higher Prices: Prices for accommodations and activities may be higher.

Autumn (March to May):

Highlights:

- Fall Foliage: Witness stunning autumn foliage as the leaves change color.

- Mild Weather: Enjoy pleasant temperatures and fewer crowds compared to summer.

- Whale Watching: Ideal time for whale-watching tours.

Considerations:

- Decreased Daylight: Days become shorter as autumn progresses, limiting outdoor activities.

- Closures: Some accommodations and services may close as the season winds down.

Winter (June to August):

Highlights:

- Snowscapes: Experience the magic of snow-covered landscapes in the Andes.

- Unique Activities: Winter opens up opportunities for skiing, snowshoeing, and other winter sports.

- Photography: Capture stunning winter scenes in Patagonia.

Considerations:

- Colder Temperatures: Expect cold and often freezing conditions, especially at higher elevations.

- Limited Accessibility: Some remote areas may be inaccessible due to snow and road closures.

- Fewer Tourists: Enjoy a quieter and less crowded Patagonia.

Perfect Seasons: Best Times to Visit

The ideal time to visit Patagonia depends on your interests and the experiences you seek. Here are recommendations for various interests:

Trekking Enthusiasts:

For trekking adventures and exploring the national parks, consider visiting during the summer months (December to February). You'll have longer daylight hours and milder temperatures for extended outdoor activities.

Wildlife Watchers:

To witness Patagonia's diverse wildlife, spring (September to November) and autumn (March to May) are excellent choices. These seasons offer opportunities to observe migratory birds, whales, and other species in their natural habitats.

Winter Sports Enthusiasts:

If you're passionate about winter sports like skiing and snowshoeing, plan your visit during the winter season (June to August). You'll find snow-covered landscapes and fewer crowds at ski resorts.

Photography Enthusiasts:

Photographers will find captivating scenes in every season. However, autumn's vibrant foliage and winter's snowy landscapes provide unique opportunities for stunning photography.

Ultimately, the best time to visit Patagonia is the one that aligns with your interests and the type of experiences you want to create. Each season offers its own charm and beauty, ensuring a memorable journey.

Unveiling Activities

Patagonia is a treasure trove of experiences and adventures waiting to be discovered. In this section, we explore the plethora of activities you can engage in during your visit:

Things to Experience: What to Do

When you're in Patagonia, the possibilities are endless. Here are some of the activities and experiences you can savor:

Hiking and Trekking:

Patagonia is renowned for its hiking trails, offering options for all skill levels. Explore the region's natural beauty by embarking on captivating hikes, such as:

- Cóndor and Eagle Viewpoints: Take in breathtaking vistas of Patagonia's landscapes.

- Laguna de los Tres: Hike to this stunning glacial lake for awe-inspiring views of the Fitz Roy massif.

- Laguna Torre: Trek to Laguna Torre for close-up views of the Cerro Torre mountain.

- Pliegue Tumbado: Reach this viewpoint for panoramic vistas of the surrounding valleys.

- Glaciar Huemul: Challenge yourself with a hike to this remote glacier.

Wildlife Observation:

Patagonia boasts diverse wildlife, and observing these creatures in their natural habitats is a captivating experience. Look out for:

- Whales: Go on a whale-watching tour to witness the majestic southern right whales.

- Penguins: Visit penguin colonies on the Patagonian coast.

- Birdwatching: Explore the region's rich birdlife, including condors, eagles, and migratory species.

- Wildlife Safaris: Join guided safaris to spot guanacos, foxes, and more.

Water Adventures:

With its numerous lakes, rivers, and fjords, Patagonia offers a range of water-based activities, such as:

- Kayaking: Paddle along serene rivers and lakes, including the Santa Cruz River.

- Boat Tours: Take boat trips to glaciers like Perito Moreno and remote estancias.

- Fishing: Try your hand at fly fishing in Patagonia's pristine waters.

Cultural Explorations:

Discover the region's rich history and culture through:

- Museums: Visit Madsen's House Museum and the Glaciarium (Ice Museum).

- Cave Explorations: Explore the Walichu cave's ancient rock art.

- City Tours: Walk through the city centers of El Calafate and Punta Arenas.

Adventures Await: Exciting Activities

While in Patagonia, prepare to embrace adventure and embark on thrilling experiences:

Mini Trekking on Ice:

Get up close and personal with glaciers by taking a mini trekking tour on the Perito Moreno Glacier. Walk on the glacier's icy surface and explore its unique features.

Kayaking the Santa Cruz River:

Navigate the pristine waters of the Santa Cruz River by kayak. Enjoy the tranquility of this scenic river as you paddle through its captivating landscapes.

Horse Riding in Estancia El Lazo:

Experience the Patagonian wilderness on horseback at Estancia El Lazo. Ride through picturesque landscapes and connect with the region's cowboy culture.

Skiing in Winter:

If you visit during the winter months, indulge in skiing and snowshoeing adventures in the snow-covered Andes, adding an exciting dimension to your Patagonian journey.

Managing Your Expenses

Traveling to Patagonia requires careful financial planning to ensure you make the most of your journey. Let's explore how to manage your expenses effectively:

Your Trip Budget: Financial Planning

Before setting off, create a detailed budget that covers all aspects of your trip, including:

- Flights: Research and book your flights well in advance to secure the best deals.

- Accommodations: Compare options, from hostels to luxury lodges, and make reservations.

- Transportation: Plan your inter-city travel, including buses, rental cars, or guided tours.

- Activities: Allocate funds for excursions, guided tours, and entrance fees to attractions.

- Meals: Budget for dining out and groceries if you plan to self-cater.

- Miscellaneous Expenses: Account for unexpected costs and souvenirs.

Cost Considerations: Staying on Track

While in Patagonia, use these strategies to manage your expenses effectively:

- Exchange Currency: Exchange currency before arriving in remote areas where ATMs may be scarce.

- Travel Insurance: Invest in comprehensive travel insurance to cover unforeseen expenses.

- Cook Meals: If budget-conscious, cook your meals in hostel kitchens or campsites.

- Group Tours: Consider group tours for cost savings, especially for excursions to remote locations.

- Shop Smart: Buy groceries and essentials in larger towns where prices are more competitive.

- Check Local Currency: Understand the exchange rate and whether businesses accept credit cards.

- Cash Reserves: Keep some cash on hand for emergencies or places that don't accept cards.

By carefully managing your expenses and planning your budget, you can fully enjoy the wonders of Patagonia without financial worries.

Our Rating System

To assist you in making informed choices during your Patagonian adventure, we've implemented a rating system to evaluate various aspects of your journey:

Evaluating Your Options: Understanding Our Ratings

Our rating system provides insights into accommodations, tours, and more. Here's what each rating signifies:

- Accommodations: Ratings for lodging options, including hostels, hotels, and lodges, range from budget-friendly to luxurious.

- Tour Experiences: Ratings for guided tours and excursions indicate their quality and value.

- Cuisine: Ratings for dining establishments, from local eateries to gourmet restaurants, reflect their offerings and ambiance.

- Transportation: Ratings for transportation options, including buses, boats, and car rentals, help you choose the most convenient and reliable ways to get around.

Making Informed Choices: Stars and Tags Explained

In addition to numerical ratings, we use stars and tags to provide additional information:

- Star Ratings: Accommodations and tours are rated on a scale of one to five stars, with five stars signifying the highest quality and comfort.

- Tags: Tags indicate specific features or attributes, such as "family-friendly," "eco-friendly," or "adventure-packed," helping you find options that align with your preferences and interests.

Our rating system aims to enhance your Patagonian journey by guiding you toward choices that suit your travel style and expectations.

Chapter 2: Exploring El Calafate

Welcome to El Calafate, an amazing location situated among Patagonia's natural scenery. We will present you with extensive information in this chapter to ensure that your trip to El Calafate is packed with memorable events.

A Look Back in Time

Let us first enjoy the historical fabric that shapes El Calafate before getting into the practical elements. Understanding the town's history broadens the scope of your exploration.

El Calafate has a rich and varied history that can be traced back to its indigenous people and later colonization. The historical backdrop lends layers of meaning to the natural beauty you'll see.

How to Get to El Calafate

Your Patagonian adventure starts with a trip to El Calafate. We'll walk you through the numerous transit alternatives, assisting you in selecting the best one for your travel style. In addition, we'll go over the best times to embark on your journey to make the most of your vacation.

Picking Your Path

El Calafate may be reached by both air and road. You have the option of flying into Comandante Armando Tola International Airport or driving through the Patagonian countryside. We'll go over the advantages and disadvantages of each option.

Optimal Timing

The timing of your visit to El Calafate might have a considerable impact on your experience. Depending on your tastes, you might like the colorful spring blooms, summer's extended daylight hours, autumn's golden colours, or winter's quiet white vistas. We'll work with you to choose the best time to visit based on your preferences.

Places to Stay

Choosing the right lodging is critical for a pleasant and comfortable stay. El Calafate has a wide choice of hotel alternatives to suit a variety of tastes and budgets. We'll go over these options in depth to help you make an informed selection.

Varieties of Accommodation

El Calafate offers a diverse range of accommodations, from modest hostels and boutique hotels to opulent resorts. Whether you're looking for a low-cost choice or a luxurious stay, we'll help you find the ideal location to rest your head.

Dining Outings

To properly experience Patagonia's spirit, you must indulge in its culinary delights. Discover a variety of dining alternatives, ranging from local gourmet treasures to international cuisine. We'll point you in the direction of the greatest restaurants to satisfy your taste buds.

Patagonian Cuisine

Discover Patagonia's distinct flavors, where traditional Argentine meals merge perfectly with locally sourced ingredients. We'll introduce you to the delectable world of Patagonian food, from juicy grilled meats to substantial stews.

Moving Around

Exploring El Calafate and its lovely environs requires easy mobility. We'll give you with useful transit information, ensuring that your excursions across this wonderful region are smooth and pleasurable.

Transportation Alternatives

Learn about the most convenient ways to get around El Calafate, whether you like to rent a car, take public transportation, or take guided tours. Each means of transportation provides a distinct perspective on the location.

Embracing El Calafate Adventures

El Calafate is brimming with exciting activities and unique experiences. Let's have a look at what you can do throughout your visit:

Glacier Perito Moreno (Walkways)

The Perito Moreno Glacier will leave you speechless. Explore the well-kept paths that provide panoramic views of this spectacular ice monster. It's an enthralling experience with one of nature's marvels.

Mini Ice Trekking + Perito Moreno Walkways

Begin a little trekking expedition on the glacier's cold surface for a closer connection with it. This exhilarating experience, paired with a visit to the walkways, immerses you in Perito Moreno's heart.

Perito Moreno Walkways + Short Navigation

Set sail on a brief navigation tour to approach the glacier's towering cliffs from the sea, followed by a leisurely exploration of the pathways for spectacular views and photo ops.

Estancia Cristina + Uppsala Glacier Navigation

Travel by boat to Estancia Cristina, a genuine Patagonian estancia, and gaze at the Uppsala Glacier. This tour combines natural beauty with historical relevance.

Estancia Cristina Navigation + Uppsala Glacier + Lodging

Extend your stay at Estancia Cristina to get the full experience. Spend the night surrounded by the tranquillity of this remote setting, and awaken to the pristine splendor of the Uppsala Glacier right outside your door.

Long Navigation to Upsala and Spegazzini Glaciers

Explore the majestic Uppsala Glacier as well as the awe-inspiring Spegazzini Glacier on an intensive sailing excursion. It's a thorough examination of Patagonia's icy beauties.

Full-Day Program at Estancia Nibepo Aike

With a full-day program at Estancia Nibepo Aike, you can immerse yourself in the true Patagonian way of life. On a typical estancia, this trip provides an in-depth look at local culture, traditions, and activities.

Day Program at Estancia Nibepo Aike

Consider the two-day program at Estancia Nibepo Aike, which includes overnight accommodations, for a more profound connection with Patagonian rural life. This comprehensive experience immerses you in the estancia lifestyle.

Estancia Nibepo Aike + Perito Moreno

Combine the allure of Estancia Nibepo Aike with a trip to the beautiful Perito Moreno Glacier for a harmonic blend of cultural immersion and natural awe.

Nibepo Aike + Southern Glaciers

Set out on an enthralling adventure across Patagonia's southern glaciers, with a wonderful stop at Estancia Nibepo Aike for a taste of warm Patagonian hospitality.

Santa Cruz River Kayaking

Paddle along the peaceful waters of the Santa Cruz River to experience peace and natural beauty. This kayaking experience provides a unique viewpoint on Patagonia's pristine landscapes, allowing you to connect deeply with nature.

Glaciarium or Ice Museum

Visit the Glaciarium or Ice Museum to learn about the amazing world of ice. Discover the region's glacial history, scientific study, and the mystery of these frozen giants through interactive exhibitions.

Cave of Walichu

Explore the old Walichu Cave, which is filled with local cave art. This site provides insight into the life and beliefs of the indigenous people who once lived in this area.

Laguna Nimez Birdwatching

Laguna Nimez is a birdwatcher's paradise, home to a wide variety of avian species. In this calm nature reserve, grab your binoculars and immerse yourself in the world of Patagonian wildlife. You'll see flamingos, swans, and a variety of other migratory and resident birds, making it a must-see for bird watchers.

El Chaltén Day Trip

Extend your Patagonian journey with a day trip to El Chaltén, a lovely community in Patagonia's center. Discover its enthralling surroundings, which include breathtaking vistas and pristine hiking routes. El Chaltén is known as the "Trekking Capital of Argentina," and you'll be able to go on breathtaking excursions across the gorgeous Andes vistas.

Walking in the City Center

Take a leisurely stroll through El Calafate's city center to take in the ambience. Discover the town's distinct character by exploring tiny stores and savoring Patagonian cuisine. It's a great opportunity to unwind after your activities and immerse yourself in the local culture.

Customized Concepts and Suggestions

We've adapted some ideas and suggestions based on the length of your stay to ensure you make the most of your time in El Calafate:

If staying for two full days

Consider seeing the Perito Moreno Glacier and its walkways on one day, followed by a day of kayaking on the Santa Cruz River on the next. This combo provides a mix of natural wonders and adventure, allowing you to get up close and personal with the glacier and Patagonia's tranquil landscapes.

If staying for four days or more

With a longer stay, you may immerse yourself in the beauty of Patagonia. Explore the glaciers of Upsala

and Spegazzini, learn about the rich culture of Estancia
Nibepo Aike, and spend the day hiking and exploring
in El Chaltén. This extended trip provides a thorough
Patagonian experience that incorporates natural beauty,
cultural immersion, and outdoor adventures.

These extensive insights and tips will ensure that your
vacation to El Calafate is packed with great
experiences and unforgettable memories. So get ready
for a fantastic tour through the heart of Patagonia.

Chapter 3: Exploring El Chaltén

Welcome to the captivating location of El Chaltén, the Trekking Capital of Argentina. In this chapter, we'll take you on a journey through the history, travel choices, accommodations, dining experiences, and exciting activities that await you in this enchanting village.

History

Before we lace up our hiking boots and hit the trails, let's dig into the historical background of El Chaltén. Understanding the village's past adds depth to your tour of this pristine wilderness.

How and When to Go

El Chaltén is a year-round destination, but the best time to visit varies on your interests. We'll guide you on the optimal times to explore this nature wonderland and help you plan your journey to perfection.

Where to Stay

Choosing the right place to rest your head is crucial for a great stay. El Chaltén offers various lodging choices, catering to different tastes and budgets. We'll provide you with insights into these places, ensuring a comfortable stay amid Patagonia's beauty.

In the Village

Discover the ease of staying right in the heart of El Chaltén, with easy access to restaurants and trails.

Hosteria el Pilar

Nestle into the peacefulness of Hosteria el Pilar, a tranquil retreat surrounded by nature.

Aguas Arriba Lodge

Experience the remote luxury of Aguas Arriba Lodge, where the wilderness is at your feet.

Domes

Find unique accommodation in eco-friendly domes, giving comfort and immersion in the natural environment.

What and Where to Eat

Patagonian food is a treat for your taste buds. We'll guide you to the best dining spots in El Chaltén, from local specialties to foreign flavors.

Moving Around

Effortless mobility is important to exploring El Chaltén and its pristine surroundings. We'll provide you with valuable information on transportation modes, ensuring your trips are smooth and enjoyable.

What to Do

El Chaltén is an outdoor enthusiast's paradise. Let's dive into the exciting activities that await you in this hiking haven:

Road to/From Calafate

Embark on a picturesque road trip between El Chaltén and El Calafate, soaking in the mesmerizing scenery along the way.

Wildlife Observation

Patagonia's wildlife is fascinating. Explore the region's fauna and spot local creatures in their natural environment.

Trekking

Hiking is at the heart of El Chaltén's appeal. We'll explore a range of trekking choices, from breathtaking viewpoints to remote glaciers:

Cóndor and Eagle Viewpoints

Hike to the Cóndor and Eagle viewpoints for panoramic vistas of the beautiful surroundings.

Hosteria Pilar + Laguna Capri

Embark on a trek that takes you to Hosteria Pilar and Laguna Capri, two captivating places.

Laguna de los Tres

Experience the awe-inspiring beauty of Laguna de los Tres and its famous views.

Laguna Torre

Hike to Laguna Torre and experience the ethereal beauty of Cerro Torre.

Pliegue Tumbado

Discover the Pliegue Tumbado trek, giving sweeping vistas of El Chaltén and its surroundings.

Glaciar Huemul

Embark on an adventure to Glaciar Huemul, a remote and beautiful glacier.

Other Trekking Alternatives

Explore additional trekking routes that cater to different skill levels and tastes.

The Road to the North and Lago del Desierto

Venture on a beautiful drive to the north, where you'll find the picturesque Lago del Desierto.

Madsen's House Museum

Discover the past of El Chaltén at Madsen's House Museum, a cultural gem.

Kayaking in Rio de las Vueltas

Paddle along the Rio de las Vueltas and soak in the serene Patagonian scenery.

Tailored Ideas and Suggestions

To make the most of your time in El Chaltén, we've tailored some ideas and tips based on the duration of your stay:

If Staying 2 Full Days

Explore the famous Laguna de los Tres and enjoy a trek to Laguna Capri on one day, followed by a journey to Laguna Torre on the next. This combination gives a mix of breathtaking views and natural wonders.

If Staying 4 Full Days or More

With an extended stay, engage yourself in the region's beauty. Experience the Pliegue Tumbado trek, visit the fascinating Glaciar Huemul, explore the road to Lago del Desierto, and enjoy a day of kayaking on the Rio de las Vueltas. This extended itinerary ensures a thorough exploration of El Chaltén's outdoor paradise.

As you start on your journey through El Chaltén, these detailed insights and ideas will enhance your experience and help you create unforgettable memories in the heart of Patagonia.

Chapter 4: Exploring Torres del Paine

Welcome to the pristine wildness of Torres del Paine National Park, one of Patagonia's most breathtaking gems. In this chapter, we will start on a journey through this iconic park, providing you with a wealth of information to ensure an unforgettable adventure.

History

Torres del Paine boasts a rich history dating back to indigenous peoples who once inhabited the area. Later, explorers and conservationists added to its legacy. Designated a UNESCO Biosphere Reserve in 1978, this park has been protected for its remarkable biodiversity and stunning landscapes.

How and when to go

Getting to Torres del Paine

To begin your Torres del Paine adventure, you'll usually start from the charming town of Puerto

Natales. From there, various transportation choices, including buses, private transfers, and even flights to nearby cities, will take you into the park.

Ideal Timing

The best time to visit Torres del Paine varies on your preferences. The peak season, from late spring to early autumn (October to April), gives pleasant weather and extended daylight hours. However, if you prefer fewer crowds and pristine landscapes, try visiting during the quieter winter months.

Where to stay

Sleeping in the Serrano area

For an intimate experience close to nature, you can opt to stay in the Serrano area. Here, you'll find cozy lodges and campsites near the southwestern park gate.

Sleeping in Puerto Natales

Puerto Natales offers a range of accommodation choices, catering to various budgets. It serves as an excellent base for your Torres del Paine exploration, with numerous trip operators and rental services available.

Within the Park Hotel Explora

Nestled in the heart of Torres del Paine, Hotel Explora offers luxury accommodations with breathtaking views. It's an ideal choice for travelers wanting both comfort and adventure.

Hotel Pehoe Overlooking Lake Pehoe, Hotel Pehoe offers a picturesque setting for your park adventure. Wake up to stunning views and easy access to hiking trails.

East of the Park Cerro Castillo

For a tranquil retreat east of the park, try Cerro Castillo. This area offers a serene atmosphere and chances to explore lesser-known trails.

Posada Tres Pasos

Immerse yourself in the Patagonian desert at Posada Tres Pasos. This remote lodge offers an off-the-grid experience surrounded by natural beauty.

Moving around

Efficient transportation is key to discovering the vast landscapes of Torres del Paine. Inside the park, you can count on tour operators, rental cars, and even horseback riding to reach different areas and trails.

What to do

Salto Grande Waterfall and Cuernos' Viewpoint

Begin your trip with a visit to Salto Grande waterfall, a natural spectacle of immense power. Nearby, the Cuernos' viewpoint gives stunning vistas of the iconic Cuernos del Paine peaks.

Lake Pehoe and Cóndor Viewpoint

Explore the mesmerizing Lake Pehoe and don't miss the chance to reach the Cóndor Viewpoint for panoramic views of the Paine Massif.

East Side of the Park Nordenskjold's Viewpoint

Discover Nordenskjold's viewpoint for a unique outlook of the park's landscapes, including its pristine lakes.

Rio Paine Waterfall

Visit the Rio Paine waterfall, where turquoise waters flow through rocky formations, creating a quiet ambiance.

Bridge over Rio Paine

Cross the bridge over Rio Paine, a great spot for photography and a peaceful pause in your trip.

Lagoon/Laguna Amarga

Explore the serene Laguna Amarga, giving picturesque surroundings and chances for birdwatching.

Trekking to Base Torres

Embark on the iconic trek to Base Torres, a difficult yet rewarding hike that leads you to the base of the magnificent Torres del Paine peaks.

Navigation to Grey Glacier

Take a boat tour to Grey Glacier and watch the mesmerizing blue ice formations up close. This trip is a must for glacier enthusiasts.

Lake Grey and Trekking

Explore the beauty of Lake Grey and consider hiking along its shores for a better look at its icy wonders.

Other Activities in the Park

Participate in activities such as horseback riding, cycling, and fishing to improve your park experience.

Visit to Puerto Natales

Explore the charming town of Puerto Natales, known for its welcoming atmosphere, local food, and vibrant culture.

Milodon Cave

Delve into the depths of Milodon Cave, where you can learn about the ancient creatures that once inhabited the area.

Navigation to Balmaceda and Serrano Glaciers

Embark on a boat tour to Balmaceda and Serrano Glaciers for a better look at these icy wonders.

Horse Riding in Estancia El Lazo

Experience the Patagonian way of life with a horseback ride adventure at Estancia El Lazo.

Some ideas and thoughts

If staying 3 full days

With three days in Torres del Paine, you can visit both iconic and lesser-known sites. Start with a walk to Base Torres on day one, followed by a visit to Grey Glacier on day two. On the third day, venture east to find Nordenskjold's viewpoint and the Rio Paine waterfall.

If staying 5 full days or more

A longer stay gives you to delve deeper into the park's beauty. Extend your trip by visiting the serene Laguna Amarga and taking a boat tour to Balmaceda and Serrano Glaciers. Additionally, discover the town of Puerto Natales and immerse yourself in its vibrant culture.

Torres del Paine beckons with its natural wonders and varied landscapes. This guide equips you with the information you need for an unforgettable trip into the heart of Patagonia's wilderness.

Chapter 6: Exploring Other Remarkable Places in Patagonia

While Patagonia is renowned for its iconic destinations, it's also a land of hidden gems and diverse landscapes. In this chapter, we'll journey beyond the well-trodden paths to explore the lesser-known but equally fascinating places and activities Patagonia has to offer.

Patagonian Atlantic Coast

Valdes Peninsula

Valdes Peninsula is a UNESCO World Heritage Site known for its astounding marine wildlife. Witness southern right whales, sea lions, and penguins in their natural habitat. Take a whale-watching tour or visit the sea lion colony at Punta Norte.

Camarones + Cabo Dos Bahías

Camarones is a charming coastal village ideal for birdwatching, especially during the breeding season when over 150 bird species can be spotted. Nearby, Cabo Dos Bahías offers stunning coastal landscapes and opportunities to see penguins and guanacos.

Bahia Bustamante

Bahia Bustamante is an eco-village where you can experience a traditional Patagonian working sheep farm. Explore its pristine beaches, seaweed fields, and diverse marine life, making it an off-the-beaten-path paradise.

Puerto Deseado

Penguin Island

Visit Penguin Island in Puerto Deseado to encounter Magellanic and rockhopper penguins. Explore the cave formations and unique geological features, making it an extraordinary destination.

Campamento Darwin / Darwin's Campsite

Campamento Darwin is a scientific station offering insights into Patagonia's natural history. Learn about local flora, fauna, and ongoing research projects, fostering a deeper understanding of the region.

Explore Puerto Deseado's diverse landscapes, including its colorful rock formations, fossil sites, and birdwatching opportunities.

Cape Horn & Fuegian Channels

Venture to Cape Horn, a legendary maritime landmark. Experience the thrill of reaching the southernmost point of South America, where the Atlantic and Pacific Oceans converge. Sail through the intricate Fuegian Channels, a maze of fjords and islands rich in history and wildlife.

Punta Arenas

City Tour

Punta Arenas offers a glimpse into Patagonian culture. Explore its historic architecture, bustling markets, and museums, including the Museo Maggiorino Borgatello, to delve into the region's heritage.

Magdalena Island

Embark on a boat trip to Magdalena Island to witness a massive colony of Magellanic penguins. The island is a protected sanctuary, allowing you to observe these charming creatures up close.

The King Penguin Colony in Useless Bay

A visit to the King Penguin Colony in Useless Bay is a unique opportunity to see the world's second-largest penguin species in their natural habitat. It's a rare and unforgettable wildlife encounter.

Patagonian Epic Roads

Route 40 (Argentina)

Route 40 is one of the longest highways globally, traversing Argentina from north to south. Journey along this iconic road, passing through diverse landscapes, charming towns, and awe-inspiring vistas.

Carretera Austral (Chile)

Carretera Austral is a scenic highway that meanders through Chilean Patagonia. Discover hidden lakes, lush forests, and remote villages along this unforgettable route.

Short Alternative in Chile

Opt for shorter sections of the Carretera Austral, perfect for a day trip or a few days of exploration.

Short Alternative through Argentina

Cross into Argentina to experience the Patagonian Andes and its picturesque landscapes.

Long Alternative

For the ultimate adventure, embark on an extended journey along the full length of the Carretera Austral.

Northwestern Patagonia

Explore the lesser-known region of Northwestern Patagonia, characterized by lush forests, pristine lakes, and captivating landscapes. Hike through national parks, visit charming towns, and discover the region's unique culture.

Chilean Channels

Skorpios Cruise

Experience the Chilean channels aboard a Skorpios Cruise. Sail through these remote waters, surrounded by stunning fjords, glaciers, and abundant marine life.

Navimag

Navimag offers an alternative way to explore the Chilean channels, allowing you to witness the untouched beauty of this remote region.

Other Activities

Fly Fishing and Hunting

Fishing

Patagonia is a world-renowned fly fishing destination, with pristine rivers and lakes teeming with trout and salmon. Engage in catch-and-release fishing experiences.

Hunting

For hunting enthusiasts, Patagonia offers opportunities for big game hunting, including deer and wild boar. Ensure you have the necessary permits and adhere to conservation regulations.

Skiing

During the winter season, Patagonia becomes a skiing paradise. Hit the slopes in resorts like Cerro Castor in Ushuaia or Cerro Catedral in Bariloche for a thrilling winter adventure.

Scuba Diving

Explore the underwater wonders of Patagonia through scuba diving. Discover kelp forests, marine life, and even shipwrecks in the region's clear, cold waters.

Golf

Play a round of golf amid stunning Patagonian landscapes. Golf courses like Llao Llao in Bariloche offer a unique sporting experience with breathtaking views.

Photography

Patagonia's landscapes are a photographer's dream. Capture the region's natural beauty, from towering peaks to serene lakes, and create lasting memories of your journey.

In this chapter, we've uncovered the hidden treasures and diverse activities that make Patagonia a remarkable destination. Whether you're a wildlife enthusiast, adventure seeker, or culture lover, Patagonia has something extraordinary to offer in every corner of its vast and awe-inspiring landscape.

Chapter 7: Patagonia Itineraries

Planning an adventure in Patagonia is a thrilling but challenging endeavor, given the vastness and diversity of the area. In this part, we offer a range of itineraries to simplify your Patagonian trip planning. Whether you have two weeks, three weeks, four weeks, or even just a winter week for whale watching, our detailed ideas will ensure an unforgettable experience.

Two Weeks (Including Travel Days)

Option 1: Argentina Only

Duration: 2 weeks

Description: Dive into Argentina's Patagonia during this two-week adventure. Start in vibrant Buenos Aires and then journey to renowned places like El Calafate, El Chaltén, and Bariloche. Engage in glacier hiking, relish breathtaking views, and soak up the rich Argentine culture.

Option 2: With Torres del Paine

Duration: 2 weeks

Description: Elevate your two-week trip by venturing into Chile's Torres del Paine National Park. Following your tour of Argentine Patagonia, cross the border to witness Torres del Paine's awe-inspiring landscapes. Embark on the iconic W Trek and meet the park's unique wildlife.

Three Weeks (Including Travel Days)

Option 1: The Big Four

Duration: 3 weeks

Description: This three-week itinerary seamlessly includes the highlights of Argentina and Chile. Discover Argentine Patagonia, visit Torres del Paine, and experience the pristine Chilean fjords and channels. Witness awe-inspiring glaciers, adorable penguins, and one-of-a-kind scenery.

Option 2: Coast and Andes, Only Argentina

Duration: 3 weeks

Description: Focus entirely on Argentina's diverse landscapes during this three-week journey. Traverse the Patagonian Atlantic coast, venture into the Andes, and discover iconic destinations such as Ushuaia and El Calafate. Immerse yourself in the region's lively culture and natural wonders.

Option 3: Mostly Chile

Duration: 3 weeks

Description: Embark on a thrilling three-week journey through Chilean Patagonia. Uncover the wonders of Torres del Paine, sail through captivating Chilean fjords, and visit remote coastal towns. Immerse yourself in Chile's unique mix of wilderness and culture.

Four Weeks (Including Travel Days)

Option 1: Grand Tour Duration: 4 weeks

Description: Experience the ultimate Patagonian adventure with this four-week grand tour that crosses both Argentina and Chile. Explore magnificent glaciers, pure fjords, enchanting national parks, and rich cultural experiences.

Option 2: Coast and Andes, Mainly Argentina

Duration: 4 weeks

Description: Delve deep into the heart of Argentine Patagonia during this four-week trip. Explore the rugged Patagonian Atlantic coast, traverse the majestic Andes, and discover hidden gems off the beaten path. Immerse yourself in local culture and the breathtaking natural beauty of the area.

Winter Week for Whale Watching

Duration: 1 week

Description: Witness the beautiful world of Patagonian whales during the winter season with a week-long trip to Peninsula Valdes. Experience the mesmerizing annual gathering of southern right whales and explore the unique marine ecosystem of this captivating area.

These comprehensive itineraries cater to diverse interests and timeframes, ensuring you craft the perfect Patagonian journey. Whether you're an outdoor enthusiast, wildlife lover, or culture explorer, Patagonia promises an array of captivating experiences waiting to be found.

© **Rick Paul**

Printed in Great Britain
by Amazon

43656604R00046